My Thoughts and Feelings

What Are You Feeling?

Sheri Lang

SOCIAL AND EMOTIONAL LEARNING FOR THE REAL WORLD™

Rosen Classroom™

I have many thoughts and feelings. They change all the time!

What do I feel today?
I think about it.

Sometimes I feel sad.
I want to cry!

I feel sad when I get hurt.

Sometimes I feel mad.
I want to yell!

I feel mad when I lose a game.

Sometimes I feel happy.
I want to smile!

I feel happy when I see my friends.

Sometimes I think sad thoughts. That makes me sad.

Sometimes I think happy thoughts.
That makes me happy again!

Words to Know

cry

smile

yell